Financial Mastery:

A Roadmap to Wealth and Security.

By

Robert Carlton

Table of Contents

Copyright © 2023 by Robert Carlton. All rights reserved.

Introduction

In an increasingly complex financial world, the quest to master your money is not just an admirable goal; it's a critical skill. This book is your comprehensive guide, whether you're starting your financial journey or looking to refine your existing knowledge.

Money management can appear daunting, filled with intricate concepts and endless decisions. However, within these pages, we demystify personal finance, providing you with a clear, manageable path to seize control of your financial future. Together, we will delve into the essentials, such as setting meaningful financial goals and constructing a budget tailored to your needs.

Our journey will lead us through the art of saving and investing, equipping you with the tools to nurture your wealth wisely. We'll also address the common challenges of debt and explore strategies for financial freedom.

But that's not all. In the pursuit of financial security, we'll uncover the world of building multiple income streams, granting you the flexibility and resilience necessary to safeguard your economic well-being.

While financial mastery doesn't transpire overnight, each step of this journey empowers you. By acquiring knowledge and adopting practical strategies, you'll become capable of informed decisions, wealth accumulation, and, ultimately, financial independence.

Are you prepared to embark on this enlightening journey? Together, we'll transform the intricacies of personal finance into a realm of opportunity and achievement. Let's begin.

Chapter 1:

Understanding Your Financial Goals

In the world of personal finance, every successful journey begins with a clear understanding of your financial goals. Your goals serve as the compass guiding your financial decisions, helping you chart a course toward the life you desire. In this chapter, we'll explore the importance of setting and defining your financial goals and how they shape your financial roadmap.

The Significance of Financial Goals

Imagine setting out on a road trip without a destination in mind. You'd likely end up lost or wandering aimlessly, unsure of where you're headed. The same principle applies to your financial journey. Without concrete goals, your financial path can become hazy and uncertain.

Financial goals provide you with purpose and direction. They give you a reason to save, invest, and make wise financial choices. Whether your goals involve buying a home, funding your children's education, retiring comfortably, or starting a business, they are the driving force behind your financial decisions.

Types of Financial Goals

Financial goals can be categorized into short-term, medium-term, and long-term objectives. Each type of goal has its own significance and requires a different approach:

1. **Short-Term Goals:** These are typically achievable within one to three years and often involve immediate needs or desires, such as building an emergency fund, paying off credit card debt, or taking a vacation.

2. **Medium-Term Goals:** These goals have a time horizon of three to ten years and may include objectives like buying a car, saving for a down payment on a house, or funding your child's college education.

3. **Long-Term Goals:** Long-term goals extend beyond a decade and encompass major life milestones, such as retirement planning, establishing financial security, and leaving a legacy for future generations.

Setting SMART Financial Goals

To make your financial goals effective, they should be SMART:

- **Specific:** Clearly define what you want to achieve. Vague goals like "I want to be rich" lack the clarity needed for actionable plans.

- **Measurable:** Establish a way to measure your progress. Quantify your goals, such as "Save $10,000 for a down payment on a house."

- **Achievable:** Ensure your goals are realistic and attainable within your current financial situation.

- **Relevant:** Your goals should align with your values and priorities. They should be meaningful to you.

- **Time-Bound:** Set a deadline for achieving your goals. A timeframe adds urgency and focus.

Creating Your Personal Financial Goals

In the upcoming sections of this chapter, we'll delve deeper into the process of creating your personal financial goals. We'll explore how to prioritize your goals, overcome common obstacles, and stay motivated on your financial journey.

Remember, understanding your financial goals is the cornerstone of financial mastery. It's the first step toward taking control of your finances and building the life you envision. So, let's dive in and discover how to set, prioritize, and pursue your financial goals effectively.

Prioritizing Your Financial Goals

Now that we recognize the significance of setting financial goals, it's time to explore the art of prioritization. In most cases, you'll have multiple goals vying for your attention. Prioritization involves deciding which goals are most important and deserve your immediate focus.

To prioritize effectively, consider the following factors:

1. Urgency: Are there goals that need to be addressed urgently? For instance, paying off high-interest debt may take precedence over saving for a luxury vacation.

2. Longevity: Long-term goals, such as retirement planning, often require early and consistent contributions. Prioritize them to benefit from compounding over time.

3. Emotional Impact: Some goals may hold significant emotional value, like providing a quality education for your children. These goals can be prioritized based on their emotional significance.

4. Financial Feasibility: Assess whether your goals are financially feasible in your current situation. This may involve adjusting your timeline or exploring alternative strategies.

Overcoming Common Goal-Setting Challenges

Setting financial goals isn't always straightforward. Challenges and uncertainties can arise, but understanding and addressing them is an essential part of the process.

Fear of Failure: Many people hesitate to set ambitious goals due to a fear of falling short. Remember that setbacks are a natural part of the journey, and learning from them is valuable.

Changing Priorities: Life circumstances change, and so do priorities. Be prepared to adjust your goals as needed but do so thoughtfully rather than impulsively.

Lack of Clarity: Sometimes, your goals may lack clarity or specificity. Take the time to refine and define your goals as you gain more insight into your financial aspirations.

Procrastination: Delaying goal setting can hinder your progress. Start today, even if your goals are preliminary. You can refine them over time.

Staying Motivated

Maintaining motivation throughout your financial journey is crucial. To keep your enthusiasm high:

Visualize Success: Create a mental image of what achieving your goals will look and feel like. Visualization can boost motivation.

Break Goals into Milestones: Divide larger goals into smaller, achievable milestones. Celebrate your successes along the way.

Stay Informed: Continuously educate yourself about personal finance. Understanding how your financial decisions impact your goals can be motivating.

Seek Support: Share your goals with a trusted friend, family member, or financial advisor. They can provide encouragement and accountability.

By understanding the importance of setting financial goals, learning how to prioritize them, overcoming challenges, and staying motivated, you're laying a solid foundation for your journey toward financial mastery.

Aligning Your Goals with Your Values

One of the fundamental principles of effective goal setting is aligning your financial goals with your core values and life aspirations. Your values are the compass that guides your decisions and actions. When your financial goals resonate with your values, you're more likely to stay committed and find purpose in your financial journey.

Consider what truly matters to you. Is it providing a secure future for your family, enjoying the freedom to travel, or making a positive impact through charitable contributions? Identifying your values helps you create meaningful goals that are personally fulfilling.

Tracking Your Progress

Setting financial goals is just the beginning. To ensure you stay on course, it's crucial to track your progress regularly. Tracking serves several important purposes:

1. **Accountability:** Regularly reviewing your progress keeps you accountable to yourself and your goals.

2. **Adjustment:** As you track your progress, you may identify areas where adjustments are needed. For instance, if you're falling behind on your savings goal, you can adapt your budget accordingly.

3. Motivation: Seeing how far you've come can boost your motivation and determination.

4. Celebration: Don't forget to celebrate your achievements, no matter how small. Celebrations reinforce your commitment to your goals.

Financial Goal Examples

To illustrate the concept of financial goals, here are a few common examples:

- **Short-Term:** Building an emergency fund, paying off credit card debt, or saving for a holiday vacation.
- **Medium-Term:** Purchasing a home, funding your child's education, or starting a small business.

- **Long-Term:** Achieving financial independence for retirement, leaving a legacy for your heirs, or making significant charitable contributions.

Your goals may be entirely unique to your life circumstances and aspirations. The key is to ensure they are specific, measurable, achievable, relevant, and time-bound (SMART).

You've embarked on a journey of self-discovery in understanding your financial goals. These goals are the compass that will guide you through the intricate world of personal finance. They will be the motivation behind your financial decisions, the backbone of your budget, and the reason you persist in building wealth.

In the chapters that follow, we'll dive deeper into each type of financial goal, providing you with practical strategies, expert insights, and real-world examples to help you achieve financial mastery. Whether your goals are short-term or long-term, small or ambitious, financial success is within your reach.

Now that you've laid the groundwork for your financial journey, let's explore the next steps together.

Chapter 2:

Budgeting Basics: Building a Strong Financial Foundation

We explored the significance of setting clear financial goals as the foundation of your financial journey. Now, we're diving into the practical side of personal finance with a critical tool that will help you reach those goals: budgeting.

Budgeting is more than just numbers; it's a tool for creating financial freedom and pursuing your dreams. Embrace it, and you'll discover that it's a powerful step toward financial mastery.

The Role of Budgeting

Budgeting is akin to the architectural blueprint of your financial house. It's a powerful tool that enables you to take control of your money, allocate resources strategically, and work towards your financial aspirations systematically.

At its core, a budget is a financial plan that outlines your income and expenses over a specified period. It empowers you to:

Track Your Money: By documenting where your money is coming from and where it's going, you gain insight into your financial habits.

Set Priorities: Budgeting helps you allocate resources to your most important financial goals and expenses.

Avoid Overspending: It serves as a guardrail, preventing you from spending more than you earn.

Build Savings: A well-structured budget includes provisions for saving and investing, helping you grow your wealth.

Creating Your Budget

Building an effective budget involves several key steps:

1. Determine Your Income: Calculate your total monthly income, including your salary, bonuses, rental income, and any other sources of revenue.

2. List Your Expenses: Categorize your expenses into fixed (e.g., rent or mortgage, utilities) and variable (e.g., groceries, entertainment). Don't forget to include periodic expenses like insurance premiums or annual subscriptions.

3. Set Financial Goals: Referencing Chapter 1, identify your financial goals. Prioritize them within your budget.

4. Allocate Funds: Assign specific amounts to each expense category, ensuring that your income covers your expenses while allowing for savings.

5. Monitor and Adjust: Regularly track your spending against your budget. Adjust your allocations as needed to stay on course.

Types of Budgets

There are various budgeting methods to choose from, each catering to different financial styles and goals:

Zero-Based Budget: In this approach, every dollar has a designated purpose, and your budget balances to zero, meaning your income minus expenses equals zero. It's a method that promotes conscious spending.

Envelope Budget: This method involves allocating physical envelopes with cash for various expense categories. When the cash in an envelope is gone, you can't spend more in that category until the next budgeting period.

Percentage-Based Budget: With this approach, you allocate a percentage of your income to specific categories. For instance, you might assign 30% to housing, 15% to transportation, and so on.

Digital Budgeting Apps: Many digital tools and apps can automate budgeting for you, making it easier to track expenses and monitor your financial health.

The Emotional Aspect of Budgeting

Budgeting isn't just about numbers; it's also about emotions and behaviours. It can bring to the surface feelings of restriction or scarcity. However, understanding these emotions and reframing your mindset about budgeting can turn it into a liberating and empowering tool.

In the following sections of this chapter, we'll delve deeper into each step of creating and managing your budget. We'll explore strategies for setting realistic spending limits, ways to handle unexpected expenses, and techniques for staying motivated on your budgeting journey.

Remember, your budget is your financial compass, guiding you toward your goals. As we proceed, you'll see how it plays a crucial role in achieving financial mastery.

Setting Realistic Spending Limits

Budgeting isn't about deprivation; it's about ensuring your money aligns with your priorities and goals. To achieve this, it's crucial to set realistic spending limits for each category in your budget. Here's how:

1. Evaluate Your Current Spending: Start by tracking your expenses for a month or two to get a clear picture of your spending patterns. This will help you identify areas where you might be overspending.

2. Prioritize Needs vs. Wants: Distinguish between essential expenses (needs) and discretionary spending (wants). Allocate a larger portion of your budget to needs, such as housing, food, utilities, and transportation.

3. Be Realistic: When setting limits for discretionary categories like dining out or entertainment, be realistic about what you can afford without straining your finances.

4. Emergency Fund: Allocate a portion of your budget to building or maintaining an emergency fund. This financial cushion will help you handle unexpected expenses without derailing your budget.

Handling Unexpected Expenses

Life is unpredictable, and unexpected expenses can disrupt even the most well-planned budget. It's essential to have strategies in place for handling these financial curveballs:

1. Emergency Fund: Having an emergency fund is like having a financial safety net. Aim to have at least three to six months' worth of living expenses saved in this fund to cover unexpected costs like medical bills or car repairs.

2. Adjust Your Budget: When an unexpected expense arises, reassess your budget and reallocate funds to accommodate it. You may need to temporarily cut back on non-essential spending to cover the unexpected cost.

3. Use Windfalls Wisely: If you receive unexpected windfalls, such as a tax refund or a work bonus, consider using a portion of these funds to replenish your emergency fund or pay off any debt.

4. Insurance: Review your insurance coverage to ensure you're adequately protected against unexpected events. This includes health insurance, auto insurance, and homeowners or renters' insurance.

Staying Motivated and Consistent

Budgeting requires discipline and consistency. Here are some tips to help you stay motivated and maintain your budget over time:

1. Regularly Review Your Budget: Set aside time each month to review your budget and track your spending. This habit helps you stay aware of your financial progress.

2. Celebrate Milestones: Celebrate your budgeting achievements, whether it's reaching a savings goal, paying off debt, or sticking to your budget for several months in a row.

3. Stay Adaptable: Life changes, and so should your budget. Don't be afraid to adjust your budget as your financial situation or goals evolve.

4. Seek Support: Share your budgeting journey with a friend or family member who can provide encouragement and accountability.

Building Savings and Investments into Your Budget

Your budget isn't just about managing expenses; it's a tool for building wealth and achieving your financial goals. Savings and investments are integral components of your budget that pave the way for a secure financial future.

The Importance of Saving

Savings are the financial cushion that shields you from unexpected expenses and provides opportunities for growth. Here's how to incorporate savings into your budget effectively:

1. Pay Yourself First: Treat your savings as a non-negotiable expense. Allocate a portion of your income to savings as soon as you receive it, just like you pay your bills.

2. Emergency Fund: Ensure your budget includes regular contributions to your emergency fund. A well-funded emergency fund provides peace of mind and financial stability.

3. Short-Term Goals: If you have short-term financial goals like a vacation or a home down payment, set up specific savings categories in your budget to fund these objectives.

Remember, your budget is the engine that drives your financial success, and the journey toward financial mastery is well underway.

Chapter 3:

Saving and Investing: Growing Your Wealth

In the previous chapters, we've established the importance of setting clear financial goals and creating a budget as the foundation of your financial journey. Now, we turn our attention to one of the most powerful wealth-building tools at your disposal: saving and investing.

The Power of Saving

Saving is the cornerstone of financial stability. It's the practice of setting aside a portion of your income for future use, whether that be for short-term goals like a vacation or for long-term objectives such as retirement. Here's why saving is essential:

Emergency Fund: Saving provides you with a financial safety net. An emergency fund covers unexpected expenses, preventing them from derailing your financial progress.

Financial Goals: Saving allows you to work towards your financial goals. Whether you're saving for a down payment on a house, your children's education, or your dream vacation, regular savings contributions get you closer to your objectives.

Peace of Mind: Knowing you have savings provides peace of mind. It reduces financial stress and gives you the confidence to handle life's uncertainties.

Strategies for Effective Saving

To make saving a consistent and effective part of your financial journey, consider these strategies:

1. Automate Your Savings: Set up automatic transfers from your checking account to your savings account. This ensures that you save a portion of your income before you have a chance to spend it.

2. Pay Yourself First: Treat savings as a non-negotiable expense in your budget. Allocate a specific percentage of your income to savings each month, just like you pay your bills.

3. Separate Savings Goals: If you have multiple savings goals, consider creating separate accounts or sub-accounts for each goal. This makes it easier to track your progress.

The Art of Investing

While saving is essential, investing is the key to growing your wealth over time. Investing involves putting your money to work in assets like stocks, bonds, real estate, and more, with the expectation of generating a return. Here's why investing is crucial:

Wealth Accumulation: Investing has the potential to generate returns that outpace inflation, allowing your money to grow and maintain its purchasing power over time.

Retirement Planning: Investing is a fundamental aspect of retirement planning. It enables you to build a nest egg that can support you during your retirement years.

Financial Goals: Whether you're saving for a home, your children's education, or other long-term goals, investing can help you reach those objectives more efficiently.

Investment Strategies

When it comes to investing, there are various strategies to consider, depending on your goals and risk tolerance:

Stock Market Investing: Investing in stocks can offer the potential for high returns over the long term. However, stocks also come with higher volatility and risk.

Bonds: Bonds are generally considered safer than stocks and provide a steady income stream through interest payments.

Real Estate: Investing in real estate, whether through property ownership or real estate investment trusts (REITs), can offer diversification and potential rental income.

Diversification: Diversifying your investments across different asset classes can help manage risk and optimize returns.

Remember, saving and investing are powerful tools for growing your wealth and achieving your financial goals.

Chapter 4:

Debt Management: Breaking Free from Financial Strain

In our journey to financial mastery, it's crucial to address one of the most significant obstacles to wealth accumulation: debt. Debt can hinder your financial progress, create stress, and limit your ability to achieve your financial goals. This chapter is dedicated to understanding and effectively managing your debt.

Understanding Types of Debt

Debt comes in various forms, and it's essential to distinguish between them. Here are the main types of debt you may encounter:

1. Good Debt vs. Bad Debt: Not all debt is created equal. Good debt is typically used to finance investments that have the potential to increase in value, such as a mortgage for a home or student loans for education. Bad debt, on the other hand, includes high-interest loans for non-essential items like credit card debt.

2. Secured vs. Unsecured Debt: Secured debt is backed by collateral, such as a home or car. If you fail to make payments, the lender can seize the collateral. Unsecured debt, like credit card debt, isn't backed by collateral but may result in legal action or damage to your credit if not repaid.

3. Fixed vs. Variable Interest Rates: Debt can have either fixed or variable interest rates. Fixed rates remain constant throughout the loan term, while variable rates can fluctuate based on market conditions.

Creating a Debt Repayment Plan

To break free from financial strain caused by debt, it's essential to create a structured debt repayment plan. Here's how to get started:

1. List Your Debts: Make a comprehensive list of all your debts, including the outstanding balance, interest rate, and minimum monthly payment for each.

2. Prioritize High-Interest Debt: Begin by addressing high-interest debt, such as credit card balances. Paying off high-interest debt first can save you money in the long run.

3. Allocate Extra Funds: Allocate any extra funds, such as bonuses, tax refunds, or windfalls, to your debt repayment. Applying additional payments can accelerate your progress.

4. Snowball or Avalanche Method: Choose a debt repayment strategy that suits your preferences. The debt snowball involves paying off the smallest debts first, while the debt avalanche focuses on the highest-interest debts.

Managing Credit Cards Wisely

Credit cards can be convenient financial tools, but they can also lead to excessive debt if not used responsibly. Here are some tips for managing credit cards wisely:

1. Pay on Time: Always make at least the minimum payment by the due date to avoid late fees and damage to your credit score.

2. Pay in Full: Whenever possible, pay your credit card balance in full each month to avoid interest charges.

3. Avoid Maxing Out: Aim to keep your credit card balances well below the credit limit. High credit utilization can negatively impact your credit score.

4. Use Rewards Wisely: If you have rewards credit cards, use the rewards wisely to benefit your financial goals, such as cashback or travel rewards.

Seeking Professional Guidance

If your debt situation is particularly challenging, consider seeking professional guidance from a credit counsellor or financial advisor. They can provide strategies and resources to help you manage and reduce your debt effectively.

Strategies for Effective Debt Management

Effective debt management goes beyond making minimum payments. It involves strategic planning and disciplined actions to eliminate debt efficiently. Here are some strategies to help you conquer your debts:

1. Create a Budget: Your budget is your ally in debt management. Allocate a portion of your income specifically for debt repayment. Ensure that you have a clear picture of your financial inflows and outflows

2. Prioritize High-Interest Debt: Start by focusing on debts with the highest interest rates. These are the ones costing you the most in interest charges. Paying them off first saves you money in the long run.

3. Consolidate and Refinance: If you have multiple high-interest debts, consider consolidating them into a single, lower-interest loan. Refinancing can reduce your overall interest burden and simplify debt management.

4. Negotiate with Lenders: In some cases, you may be able to negotiate with your creditors for lower interest rates, extended payment terms, or even partial debt forgiveness. Don't hesitate to reach out and discuss your options.

5. Automate Payments: Set up automatic payments for your debts to ensure you never miss a due date. Timely payments are crucial for maintaining a good credit score.

6. Cut Unnecessary Expenses: Temporarily reduce discretionary spending to free up more money for debt repayment. Every extra dollar you put toward debt brings you closer to financial freedom.

7. Snowball or Avalanche Method: Choose a debt repayment strategy that suits your psychology. The debt snowball method involves paying off the smallest debts first, providing quick wins and motivation. The debt avalanche method prioritizes high-interest debts for maximum interest savings.

Maintaining Financial Health

While focusing on debt repayment, it's important to maintain overall financial health:

1. Emergency Fund: Continue building or maintaining your emergency fund. This financial cushion prevents unexpected expenses from derailing your debt repayment plan.

2. Retirement Savings: Don't neglect your retirement savings, especially if your employer offers a retirement plan with matching contributions. Contribute enough to get the full match, as this is essentially free money for your future.

3. Insurance: Review your insurance coverage to ensure you're adequately protected. Health, auto, and homeowner's or renter's insurance can safeguard you from unexpected financial setbacks.

4. Seek Professional Advice: If your debt situation is complex or overwhelming, consider consulting with a financial advisor or credit counsellor. They can provide tailored guidance and strategies for your specific circumstances.

Remember that the journey to financial mastery involves not only eliminating debt but also building wealth and security. Keep in mind that responsible debt management is a crucial step toward achieving your long-term financial goals and securing your financial future.

Chapter 5:

Expense Optimization: Maximizing Savings

As we progress on the path to financial mastery, we recognize that managing expenses plays a pivotal role in achieving our financial goals. In this chapter, we'll delve into strategies for optimizing your expenses and maximizing your savings.

The Importance of Expense Optimization

Expense optimization involves evaluating your spending habits and making conscious choices to reduce unnecessary or wasteful expenses. Here's why it matters:

1. Increased Savings: When you cut unnecessary expenses, you free up more money for savings and investments, accelerating your progress toward financial goals.

2. Financial Flexibility: Expense optimization provides greater financial flexibility. You'll have the resources to handle unexpected expenses, explore new opportunities, or invest in experiences that matter to you.

3. Reduced Stress: A well-organized budget with optimized expenses can reduce financial stress and provide peace of mind.

Identifying Opportunities for Savings

To start optimizing your expenses, follow these steps:

1. Review Your Spending: Analyze your recent financial statements, receipts, and transactions. Categorize your spending into essential (needs) and non-essential (wants) expenses.

2. Set Priorities: Determine your financial priorities and align your spending accordingly. Focus on what matters most to **you and your long-term goals.**

3. Cut Unnecessary Expenses: Identify expenses that don't align with your priorities or offer little value. These can include subscription services you rarely use, dining out excessively, or impulse purchases.

4. Negotiate Regular Bills: Explore opportunities to negotiate bills such as insurance premiums, cable or internet charges, and even interest rates on loans or credit cards.

Creating an Expense Optimization Plan

Once you've identified areas for potential savings, it's time to create a practical expense optimization plan:

1. Set Savings Goals: Establish specific savings goals and allocate a portion of your budget to each one. This could include emergency savings, retirement contributions, or saving for a major purchase.

2. Track Your Spending: Use budgeting tools or apps to track your expenses and monitor your progress. Many apps categorize spending automatically, making it easier to see where your money goes.

3. Reduce Discretionary Spending: Prioritize needs over wants. Reduce discretionary spending, such as entertainment and dining out, and reallocate those funds to your savings goals.

4. Automate Savings: Set up automatic transfers from your checking account to your savings or investment accounts. This ensures you save consistently.

Efficient Grocery Shopping

One area where expense optimization can have a significant impact is grocery shopping. Here are some tips for efficient grocery shopping:

1. Plan Your Meals: Create a weekly meal plan and shopping list based on what you intend to cook. This prevents impulse purchases and reduces food waste.

2. Use Coupons and Discounts: Look for coupons, discounts, and loyalty programs at your grocery store. These can lead to substantial savings over time.

3. Buy Generic Brands: In many cases, store-brand or generic products are just as good as name brands but come at a lower price.

4. Avoid Impulse Buys: Stick to your shopping list and avoid adding items to your cart on a whim. Impulse buys can quickly inflate your grocery bill.

Expense optimization is a dynamic process that involves continuous evaluation and adjustment of your spending habits. By consistently optimizing your expenses, you can maximize your savings and create a solid financial foundation.

Chapter 6:

Retirement Planning: Securing Your Future

In this chapter, we'll delve into the essential topic of retirement planning, a crucial aspect of achieving financial security and ensuring a comfortable retirement.

Understanding the Importance of Retirement Planning

Retirement is a significant life milestone, and planning for it is essential for several reasons:

1. Maintaining Financial Independence: Retirement planning allows you to maintain financial independence and avoid relying solely on government benefits or family support during your retirement years.

2. Maintaining Your Lifestyle: Proper planning ensures that you can continue to enjoy the lifestyle you desire, including travel, hobbies, and leisure activities.

3. Peace of Mind: Knowing that you have a secure financial future provides peace of mind, reducing anxiety about your retirement years.

Key Components of Retirement Planning

Successful retirement planning involves several key components:

1. Determining Retirement Goals: Start by envisioning your ideal retirement lifestyle. Do you plan to travel, pursue hobbies, or volunteer? Understanding your goals will help you estimate your retirement expenses.

2. Calculating Retirement Income Needs: Estimate your retirement income needs based on your expected expenses and desired lifestyle. Consider factors such as housing, healthcare, and leisure activities.

3. Building Retirement Savings: Contribute regularly to retirement accounts such as 401(k)s, IRAs, or other tax-advantaged accounts. Take advantage of employer-sponsored retirement plans and consider additional investments.

4. Asset Allocation: Diversify your retirement portfolio to manage risk. Depending on your risk tolerance and time horizon, allocate assets to stocks, bonds, and other investment options.

5. Minimizing Taxes: Be mindful of tax implications in retirement. Consider strategies to minimize taxes on retirement withdrawals, such as Roth conversions and tax-efficient investment strategies.

6. Social Security and Pensions: Understand how Social Security and any pension plans will contribute to your retirement income. Optimize your claiming strategy to maximize benefits.

Healthcare and Long-Term Care Considerations

Healthcare is a significant expense in retirement, and planning for it is crucial:

1. Medicare: Understand the basics of Medicare, including when you're eligible and the different parts of the program. Plan for Medicare premiums and out-of-pocket costs.

2. Long-Term Care: Consider the potential need for long-term care and explore options for covering these costs, such as long-term care insurance.

Monitoring and Adjusting Your Plan

Retirement planning is an ongoing process:

1. Regular Reviews: Periodically review your retirement plan to ensure it aligns with your goals and financial situation. Adjust as needed.

2. Emergency Funds: Maintain an emergency fund even in retirement to cover unexpected expenses without disrupting your retirement income.

3. Stay Informed: Stay informed about changes in tax laws, retirement account rules, and investment options that may affect your retirement plan.

As you proceed through your retirement planning journey, remember that securing your financial future is a gradual process that requires dedication and foresight.

Chapter 7:

Conclusion - The Path to Financial Mastery

Congratulations on reaching the conclusion of this journey towards financial mastery. In this final chapter, we'll summarize the key principles and steps you've learned throughout this book and reflect on the path ahead.

Recap of Key Principles

1. Financial Goals: Setting clear and achievable financial goals is the foundation of your financial journey. These goals give purpose to your efforts and help you stay motivated.

2. Budgeting: Creating and sticking to a budget is essential for managing your finances effectively. It allows you to allocate your income toward your priorities and track your progress.

3. Savings and Investments: Building a strong financial foundation involves regular saving and smart investing. Savings provide security and opportunities, while investments grow your wealth over time.

4. Debt Management: Responsible debt management is crucial for financial freedom. Strategies like prioritizing high-interest debt and negotiating with lenders can help you break free from financial strain.

5. Expense Optimization: Optimizing your expenses involves evaluating your spending habits, prioritizing needs over wants, and reallocating funds to your financial goals.

6. Multiple Income Streams: Diversifying your income sources enhances your financial security and wealth-building potential. Side hustles, investments, and passive income can all contribute to multiple income streams.

7. Retirement Planning: Preparing for retirement ensures that you can maintain your desired lifestyle and enjoy financial independence in your golden years. It involves setting goals, saving consistently, and understanding healthcare and long-term care considerations.

The Ongoing Journey

Remember that financial mastery is a lifelong journey. Your financial goals and circumstances may evolve, and your strategies should adapt accordingly. Here are some key takeaways for your ongoing financial journey:

1. Regular Reviews: Periodically review your financial goals, budget, and investment portfolio. Make adjustments as needed to stay on track.

2. Emergency Fund: Maintain an emergency fund to handle unexpected expenses without derailing your financial plans.

3. Professional Guidance: Consider seeking advice from financial advisors or experts when faced with complex financial decisions or life changes.

4. Lifelong Learning: Stay informed about financial trends, investment options, and tax laws. Continuous learning empowers you to make informed financial choices.

5. Balance and Enjoyment: While financial goals are essential, remember to enjoy life along the way. Budget for experiences and moments that bring happiness and fulfilment.

Conclusion: A Journey Worth Taking

Your journey to financial mastery is not just about numbers; it's about securing your future, achieving your dreams, and gaining peace of mind. By implementing the principles and steps outlined in this book, you're well on your way to financial success.

Financial mastery is not a destination but an ongoing process. Embrace the challenges and opportunities that come your way, and continue building the wealth and security you desire. Your financial future is in your hands, and with dedication and smart financial choices, you can shape it to align with your goals and aspirations.

Thank you for embarking on this journey with us. May your financial path be filled with prosperity, wisdom, and fulfillment.